BEARING ARMS AND TRAGEDY

2011 TUCSON SHOOTING AND GUN CONTROL

Virginia Loh-Hagan

45TH PARALLEL PRESS

Published in the United States of America by Cherry Lake Publishing
Ann Arbor, Michigan
www.cherrylakepublishing.com

Reading Adviser: Beth Walker Gambro, MS, Ed., Reading Consultant, Yorkville, IL
Cover Designer: Felicia Macheske

Photo Credits: © Bobby Stevens Photo/Shutterstock.com, cover, 1; © Peter Carney/Shutterstock.com, 5; © Prath/
Shutterstock.com, 6; © Usa-Pyon/Shutterstock.com, 12; © Jeffery Hewitt/Shutterstock.com, 17; © Christopher
Penler/Shutterstock.com, 19; © J. Louis Bryson/Shutterstock.com, 21; © Phil Pasquini/Shutterstock.com, 22;
© Nicole S Glass/Shutterstock.com, 25; © Rob Crandall/Shutterstock.com, 29

Graphic Elements Throughout: © Chipmunk131/Shutterstock.com; © Nowik Sylwia/Shutterstock.com;
© Andrey_Popov/Shutterstock.com; © NadzeyaShanchuk/Shutterstock.com; © KathyGold/Shutterstock.com;
© Black creator/Shutterstock.com; © Edvard Molnar/Shutterstock.com; © Elenadesign/Shutterstock.com;
© estherpoon/Shutterstock.com

45th Parallel Press is an imprint of Cherry Lake Publishing.

Library of Congress Cataloging-in-Publication Data
Names: Loh-Hagan, Virginia, author.
Title: Bearing arms and tragedy : 2011 Tucson shooting and gun control / by Virginia Loh-Hagan.
Description: Ann Arbor, Michigan : Cherry Lake Publishing, 2022. | Series: Behind the curtain
Identifiers: LCCN 2021037475 | ISBN 9781534199521 (hardcover) | ISBN 9781668900666 (paperback) |
    ISBN 9781668902103 (pdf) | ISBN 9781668906422 (ebook)
Subjects: LCSH: Gun control—Arizona—Tucson—Juvenile literature. | Mass shootings—Arizona—Tucson—Juvenile
    literature.
Classification: LCC HV7438.T83 L64 2022 | DDC 364.152/3409791776—dc23
LC record available at https://lccn.loc.gov/2021037475

Cherry Lake Publishing would like to acknowledge the work of the Partnership for 21st Century Learning,
a Network of Battelle for Kids. Please visit *http://www.battelleforkids.org/networks/p21* for more information.

Printed in the United States of America
Corporate Graphics

A Note on Dramatic Retellings

Participating in Readers Theater, or dramatic retellings, can greatly improve reading skills, especially fluency. The books in the **BEHIND THE CURTAIN** series give readers opportunities to learn about important historical events in a fun and engaging way. These books serve as a bridge to more complex texts. All the characters and stories have been fictionalized. To learn more, check out the Perspectives Library series and the Modern Perspectives series, as **BEHIND THE CURTAIN** books are aligned to these stories.

TABLE of CONTENTS

HISTORICAL BACKGROUND

Gabby Giffords is from Tucson, Arizona. Giffords survived a shooting. Today, she is an activist. She fights for gun control.

She served as a U.S. Representative. She liked to meet with her constituents. She hosted "Congress on Your Corner" meetings. She met with people in Tucson. On January 8, 2011, she met them in a Safeway parking lot. Safeway is a grocery store chain.

A gunman targeted Giffords. He planned to kill her. He went to the Tucson Safeway. He took out a semiautomatic weapon. He shot Giffords in the head. Then he shot at others. Including Giffords, he shot 19 people. Six of them died. Giffords and 12 other people were hurt.

Vocabulary

activist (AK-tih-vist) a person who fights for political or social change

constituents (kuhn-STICH-ooh-uhnts) voting members of a community

semiautomatic (seh-mee-ah-tuh-MA-tik) capable of firing one shot every time the trigger is pulled

FLASH FACT!

A planned murder for political reasons is an assassination.

Vocabulary

bystanders (BYE-stan-duhrz) people who are present at an event

magazine (MA-guh-zeen) a device that stores bullets for guns

Bystanders stopped the gunman. Roger Salzgeber grabbed a folding chair. He hit the gunman in the back of the head. Bill Badger tackled the gunman and got him on the ground. The gunman dropped the gun magazine. Patricia Maisch grabbed it. Other people helped. They held him down. The police came and took the gunman away.

Giffords was rushed to the hospital. The bullet broke her skull. It hit the left side of her brain. Giffords almost died. She survived. But she had to relearn how to walk and talk.

Shootings continue in the United States. Many people want to change our gun laws.

CAST of CHARACTERS

NARRATOR: person who helps tells the story

KASEY: an **eyewitness** who was at the Tucson shooting in 2011 and who attended the 2011 memorial

SAM: a young male student who attended the 2011 memorial

MARIAN: a young female student who attended the 2011 memorial and the 2018 March for Our Lives

TONY: a young male student who attended the 2018 March for Our Lives

ALEXA: a young female student at Marjory Stoneman Douglas High School who attended the 2018 March for Our Lives

SPOTLIGHT
AMPLIFICATION OF AN ACTIVIST

Jazmine Wildcat is Native American. She is a member of the Northern Arapaho tribe. She lives in the Wyoming area. She fights for safer gun laws. She wants to protect young people from violence. She said, "We cannot just sit here and wait for the next violent event to happen." She writes letters to lawmakers. She fights for background checks. She said, "If you're a responsible gun owner, you shouldn't have to mind having to do the extra check to get a gun. More checks. Background checks, mental health checks." She has a personal connection to this issue. Her grandfather fought in the Vietnam War (1959–1975). He suffered mental trauma. He threatened to take his life with a gun. She and her family members had to take away his gun. She thought, because of his mental state, he shouldn't have been able to get a gun in the first place.

Vocabulary
eyewitness (eye-WIT-nuhss)
a person who has personally seen
something happen

FLASH FACT!
Some people own guns for safety. Others buy them for hunting, gun collecting, or work reasons.

ACT 1

NARRATOR: *It's January 12, 2011. It's 4 days after the Tucson shooting. A **memorial** is taking place at the University of Arizona campus. **KASEY**, **SAM**, and **MARIAN** are there.*

KASEY: I like the name of this memorial.

SAM: "Together We Thrive: Tucson and America."

MARIAN: We can remember the victims. We can heal together. We can unite as a nation.

KASEY: I'll never forget that day.

MARIAN: You were there?

KASEY: Yes. I still have nightmares about it. I can still hear the popping sounds. I can still smell the gunpowder.

MARIAN: That sounds awful.

KASEY: There was so much blood. Everyone was screaming. So many people got hurt.

SAM: What would make someone do such a thing?

MARIAN: It doesn't matter. There is no good reason for shooting people. It was senseless.

Vocabulary
memorial (muh-MOHR-ee-uhl) an event or object serving to remember something or someone

FLASH FACT!
The memorial was on TV. President Obama gave a speech. More than 30 million Americans watched.

NARRATOR: *There are pictures of all the victims. Six people died. Kasey, Sam, and Marian are looking at their pictures. They read the picture* **captions**. *They honor each victim. They say their names out loud.*

KASEY: Phyllis Schneck was 79 years old. She was a **homemaker**. She volunteered in her church. She baked the best macaroni and cheese. She made beautiful quilts.

SAM: Dorothy Morris was 76 years old. She was a **retired** secretary. She loved to travel and cook.

MARIAN: Dorwan Stoddard was 76 years old. He was a retired construction worker. He protected his wife. He pushed her to the ground. He shielded her with his body.

KASEY: John Roll was 63 years old. He was a U.S. district judge. He played the guitar. He loved to swim.

Vocabulary

captions (KAP-shuhnz) brief explanations of what is in a photo

homemaker (HOH-may-kuhr) someone who manages a home

retired (rih-TYE-uhrd) having left one's job and stopped working

FLASH FACT!

Say the names of victims. Avoid saying the names of shooters.

SAM: Gabe Zimmerman was 30 years old. He worked for Giffords. He was part of her staff. He was engaged to be married. He liked to hike.

MARIAN: Christina-Taylor Green was 9 years old. She was born on September 11, 2001. She liked baseball.

KASEY: My daughter is 9 years old.

MARIAN: My little sister went to school with Christina-Taylor.

SAM: I could've been there. My mom wanted to go to the store. She needed food to make dinner. Luckily, we decided to eat out instead.

MARIAN: That's what's scary about this. Shootings could happen at any time.

KASEY: Mass shootings happen more than they should. But they are still rare.

SPOTLIGHT
A SPECIAL EFFECT

Hadiya Pendleton was killed in 2013. She was a 15-year-old Black girl. She lived in Chicago, Illinois. On January 29, after school, she went to a local park. She was standing with friends. Two gang members shot her in the back. They thought she was someone else. The Pendleton family became gun control activists. They started an organization called #WearOrange. They encourage people to wear orange on the first Friday in June. This honors Pendleton's birthday, June 2. Wearing orange means standing against gun violence. Orange was chosen on purpose. Hunters wear orange to protect themselves. Orange is bright. Other hunters can see it. The Pendleton family states, "We wear orange to be seen, and demand that we be heard."

Vocabulary
mass shootings
(MASS SHOO-tings) shootings in which at least 4 people are shot

FLASH FACT!
The Christina-Taylor Green Memorial Park is in Tucson. It has a sculpture of Christina-Taylor.

MARIAN: One mass shooting is one too many. It's still scary.

KASEY: We can't live our lives in fear. We can't let them win.

SAM: That's why we need to protect the Second Amendment.

MARIAN: What's that?

SAM: It states that a **militia** is necessary for national security. It also states that we have the right to **bear arms**.

MARIAN: More guns is not the answer. I think we should have fewer guns.

SAM: My family owns a gun shop. Guns are for protection. They're not for violence.

MARIAN: Guns are the reason why people died.

SAM: If more people had guns, maybe the gunman could have been stopped. A good guy with a gun can stop a bad guy with a gun.

MARIAN: Only soldiers should have guns. Citizens shouldn't walk around with guns. That makes me nervous.

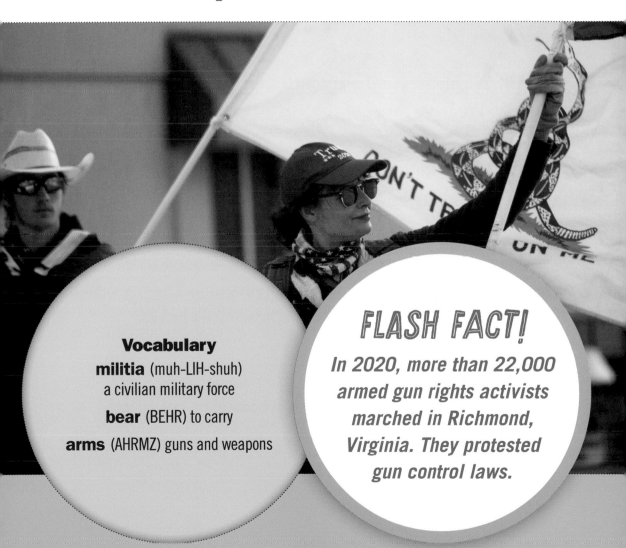

Vocabulary

militia (muh-LIH-shuh) a civilian military force

bear (BEHR) to carry

arms (AHRMZ) guns and weapons

FLASH FACT!

In 2020, more than 22,000 armed gun rights activists marched in Richmond, Virginia. They protested gun control laws.

SAM: Some people want to protect their homes. Some people need to hunt for food.

KASEY: No **civilian** should have semiautomatic weapons. That doesn't make sense.

SAM: But we have the right to carry guns.

MARIAN: We also have the right to life. We have the right to liberty. We have the right to **pursue** happiness.

KASEY: There should be more gun control. There should be more gun safety laws.

SAM: We're careful at our gun shop. People need to be trained. They need to know how to use guns. They need to know how not to use guns. They also can't have a mental health disorder.

MARIAN: Mental health is also a big concern. We should be providing more services.

KASEY: Most people with mental illnesses are never violent. It's important to not blame mental illnesses.

Vocabulary

civilian (suh-VIL-yuhn) a person who is not in the military

pursue (puhr-SOO) to seek

FLASH FACT!

Most violence is committed by people without mental illnesses. Blaming mental illnesses is distracting. It takes attention away from gun control issues.

ACT 2

NARRATOR: *It's March 24, 2018. The March for Our Lives is taking place. This is a student-led protest in Washington, D.C. It is supporting gun control.* **TONY, ALEXA,** *and* **MARIAN** *are at the march.*

TONY: There are so many people here.

ALEXA: There are more than 800 other events. These events are all happening at the same time. They're happening all over the world.

MARIAN: I bet more than 2 million people are participating. It'll be one of the largest protests in U.S. history.

TONY: That's amazing. But the reason why we're here is sad.

ALEXA: I go to Marjory Stoneman Douglas High School. It's in Parkland, Florida.

MARIAN: What a terrible **tragedy**.

Vocabulary
tragedy (TRA-juh-dee)
an event causing great suffering

FLASH FACT!

Social media increased awareness. #MarchForOurLives was used more than 3.6 million times.

ALEXA: The shooting happened on February 14, 2018. Luckily, I was out sick that day.

TONY: I still can't believe that happened. How could a gunman open fire in a school?

FLASH FACT!

The Parkland shooting is the deadliest high school shooting in U.S. history.

ALEXA: Seventeen people were killed. Seventeen others were hurt. I knew them. Our entire community was heartbroken. We lost friends. We lost family members.

MARIAN: Let's say their names.

ALEXA: These are the students who were killed: Alyssa Alhadeff, Martin Duque Anguiano, Nicholas Dworet, Jaime Guttenberg, Luke Hoyer, Cara Loughran, Gina Montalto, Joaquin Oliver, Alaina Petty, Meadow Pollack, Helena Ramsay, Alex Schachter, Carmen Schentrup, and Peter Wang.

TONY: These are the teachers and staff who were killed: Scott Beigel, Aaron Feis, and Chris Hixon.

MARIAN: I went to the Tucson Shooting Memorial. That was in 2011. I said the victims' names there.

ALEXA: Too many people have died. These shootings are so senseless.

MARIAN: That's why I'm here. I have been **advocating** for gun control. I've been doing this for the past 7 years.

TONY: I came to learn more. I saw the Parkland shooting on the news. I wanted to do something.

ALEXA: I came to support my friends. The Parkland student survivors became activists. They planned this march. They formed an activist group. The group is called "Never Again MSD."

TONY: What does MSD mean?

ALEXA: Marjory Stoneman Douglas. It's the name of our high school. We don't want people to forget. Emma Gonzalez is a Parkland survivor. She said, "We are going to be the last mass shooting."

MARIAN: I hope that's true. But I fear it's not. As long as people have guns, there will be shootings.

Vocabulary

advocating (AD-vuh-kay-ting) fighting for a cause or a change

FLASH FACT!

Florida passed a law called the Marjory Stoneman Douglas High School Public Safety Act.

ALEXA: Hopefully, this march results in **reform**.

TONY: What are some things we're fighting for?

MARIAN: First, there should be laws about who can buy guns. Gun sellers should require universal background checks. They need to check people's histories. Some people shouldn't be allowed to buy guns. This includes people with violent histories and people with criminal histories.

TONY: It would take time to process the background checks. I assume there's a fee for this too. It would be harder to get guns. This gives more people time to think. They can think about if they really need a gun or not.

ALEXA: Some gun buyers get around the background checks. We also want to get rid of these **loopholes**.

TONY: What do you mean?

NRA stands for National Rifle Association. It was founded in 1871. It's the major supporter of gun rights. It's a powerful group. Today, its members fight against gun control laws. But the NRA has a history of supporting gun control. It supported the Gun Control Act of 1968. This law required gun sellers to have permits. It also banned criminals and those with mental disorders from owning guns. They also believe owning guns is a civil right. This makes the NRA the oldest civil rights organization in the United States. NRA members have supported the civil rights movement. Some members helped train Black people to protect themselves. The NRA still provides training programs. It trains civilians and police officers. The NRA has an Eddie Eagle GunSafe program. This program promotes gun safety to young children.

Vocabulary
reform (rih-FORM) change
loopholes (LOOP-holz) ways of getting out of following rules

FLASH FACT!
Many people made signs for the march. Signs read, "Protect kids, not guns!"

ALEXA: Some people buy guns at gun shows. Private gun show sellers don't require background checks.

TONY: I see why people want guns. Getting guns is an individual choice. But background checks make sense to me. What are some other issues?

ALEXA: Kids don't need guns. We want to raise the **federal** age of gun ownership from 18 to 21.

TONY: There are age rules for other things. It makes sense to have an age rule for gun ownership.

MARIAN: We should also ban **assault weapons**. This includes semiautomatic guns. This includes magazines and **bump stocks**.

TONY: I can understand why the military needs assault weapons. The military defends our country. But civilians don't need them.

MARIAN: In my perfect world, no one would need guns.

ALEXA: There'd be no more shootings.

TONY: There'd be no more violence.

MARIAN: Never again.

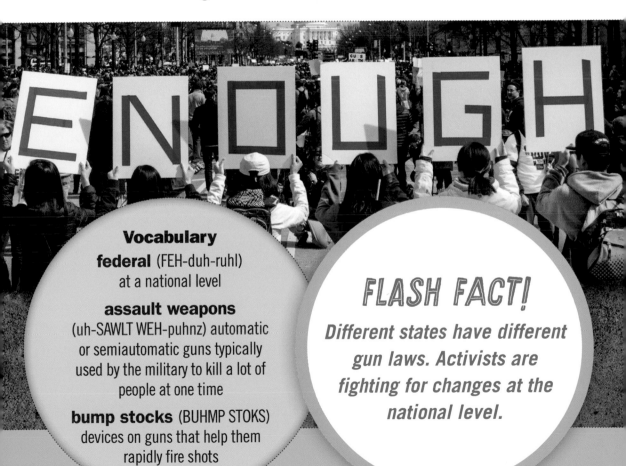

Vocabulary

federal (FEH-duh-ruhl) at a national level

assault weapons (uh-SAWLT WEH-puhnz) automatic or semiautomatic guns typically used by the military to kill a lot of people at one time

bump stocks (BUHMP STOKS) devices on guns that help them rapidly fire shots

FLASH FACT!

Different states have different gun laws. Activists are fighting for changes at the national level.

FLASH FORWARD
CURRENT CONNECTIONS

The Tucson shooting happened in 2011. But its legacy lives on. We are still feeling its effects. There is still so much work for us to do.

- **Stop gun violence:** Gun violence has increased. The year 2020 was one of the deadliest years. Almost 20,000 people in the United States were killed by gun violence in 2020. COVID-19 broke out in spring 2020. There was racial unrest during the summer of 2020. Gun sales increased in record numbers in 2020. It's important to be safe and smart about guns.

- **Reform the police:** Racial unrest was common in 2020. George Floyd was a Black man living in Minnesota. On May 25, he was killed. A police officer knelt on his neck for about 9 minutes. His last words were, "I can't breathe." Other Black people were killed by police in recent years. They include Breonna Taylor, Michael Brown, Stephon Clark, Alton Sterling, and Atatiana Jefferson. Black Lives Matter believes the officers acted unjustly. They want police to stop using deadly force against people of color. It is important to end racist police practices.

- **Stop anti-Asian hate:** Hate crimes against those with Asian backgrounds increased by 150 percent in 2020. Some people blamed the COVID-19 virus on anyone with an Asian background. On March 16, 2021, there were shootings in Atlanta, Georgia. Six Asian American women were killed. Their names were Xiaojie Tan, Daoyou Feng, Hyun Jung Grant, Soon Chung Park, Suncha Kim, and Yong Ae Yue. Other non-Asian victims were Paul Andre Michels and Delaina Ashley Yaun González. It is important to fight White supremacy.

CONSIDER THIS!

TAKE A POSITION! Gun rights versus gun control? This issue is not simple. Some people think owning guns is one of our civil rights. Other people think owning guns is dangerous. Should civilians have guns? Argue your point with reasons and evidence.

SAY WHAT? The March for Our Lives was student-led. There are many examples of student activism. Do more research. Describe an example.

THINK ABOUT IT! Think about these facts: Black men are affected by gun violence the most. A White American is twice as likely to own a gun than a Black American. How is the gun issue racialized? What stereotypes do you have?

Learn More

Bajramovic, Hana. *Whose Right Is It? The Second Amendment and the Fight Over Guns.* New York, NY: Henry Holt and Company, 2020.

Doeden, Matt. *Gun Violence: Fighting for Our Lives and Our Rights.* Minneapolis, MN: Lerner Publishing, 2020.

Orr, Tamra B. *Tucson Shooting and Gun Control.* Ann Arbor, MI: Cherry Lake Publishing, 2018.

Smith, Elliot. *Gun Violence and the Fight for Public Safety.* Minneapolis, MN: Lerner Publishing, 2022.

INDEX

ABOUT THE AUTHOR

Dr. Virginia Loh-Hagan is an author, former K-8 teacher, curriculum designer, and university professor. She's currently the director of the Asian Pacific Islander Desi American (APIDA) Center at San Diego State University. She works on a school campus. So, she is committed to school safety. She lives in San Diego with her one very tall husband and two very naughty dogs.